A CLASSIC BIBLE CHAPTER

EPHESIANS 6

Putting On The Full Armor Of God

by

Allen C. Liles
Liles Communications, LLC

Ephesians 6
Putting On The Full Armor Of God

By

Allen C. Liles
Liles Communications, LLC

Published By
Positive Imaging, LLC
bill@positive-imaging.com

All Rights Reserved

No part of this publication may be reproduced in whole or in part, or stored in a retrieval system, or transmitted in any form or by any means, electronic, mechanical, printing, photocopying, recording or otherwise without written permission from the publisher, except for the inclusion of brief quotations in a review. For information regarding permission, contact the publisher.

Copyright   2020   Allen C. Liles
ISBN: 9781951776466

This book is dedicated to my dear wife
and partner in ministry
Jan Carmen Liles

(1941-2017) RIP

EPHESIANS 6

"Finally be strong in the Lord and in his mighty power. Put on the full armor of God, so that you can take your stand against the devil's schemes. (Ephesians 6:10-11)

Contents

Key Verses of Ephesians 6	11
Introduction	13
The Apostle Paul	17
Inner Preparations For Study of Ephesians 6	21
NIV Bible Text	23
Commentary	27
Ephesians 6: 1-4	
Instructions To Children and Parents	
Ephesians 6: 5-9	31
Instructions To Slaves and Masters	
Ephesians 6: 10-11	35
Putting On The Full Armor of God	
Ephesians 6: 12	39
Who We Struggle Against	
Ephesians 6: 13	41
Standing Our Ground Against Evil	
Ephesians 6: 14	43
The Belt of Truth and Breastplate of Righteousness	
Ephesians 6: 15	45
Our Feet Fitted With Readiness From The Gospel of Peace	

Ephesians 6: 16   47
  The Shield of Faith
Ephesians 6: 17   49
The Helmet of Salvation and Sword of The Spirit
Ephesians 6: 18   51
  Praying In The Spirit
Ephesians 6: 19-20   53
 Pray For The Ambassador In Chains
Ephesians 6: 21-24   55
Encouragement, Peace, Love, Faith and Grace To All Who Love Jesus
Other Important Verses In Paul's Letter To The Ephesians   59
What About Ephesus?   63
God Visits Paul In Prison   67
A Fantasy of Paul's Thoughts Before Martyrdom   73
A Fantasy of Nero's Thoughts   79
Twelve Gifts Of Ephesians 6   83
Belinda's Quandary   89
Most Common Types of Spiritual Attacks   101
Conclusion   103
A Few Last Words From Paul   105
Notes   111

KEY VERSES OF EPHESIANS 6

"Children, obey your parents in the LORD, for this is right. Honor your father and mother—which is the first commandment with a promise—so that it may go well with you and that you may enjoy long life on the earth." (Ephesians 6: 1-3)

"Fathers, do not exasperate your children. Instead, bring them up in the training and instruction of the Lord." (Ephesians 6:4)

"Finally, be strong in the Lord and in his mighty power." (Ephesians 6:10)

"Put on the full armor of God, so that you can take your stand against the devil's schemes. For our struggle is not against flesh and blood, but against the rulers, against the authorities, against the powers of this dark world and against the spiritual forces of evil in the heavenly realms." (Ephesians 6: 11-12)

"Therefore, put on the full armor of God, so that when the day of evil comes, you may be able to stand your ground, and after you have done everything, to stand."
(Ephesians 6:13)

"Stand firm then, with the belt of truth buckled around your waist, and the breastplate of righteousness in place. And with your feet fitted with the readiness that comes from the gospel of peace." (Ephesians 6:14-15)

"In addition to all this, take up the shield of faith, with which you can extinguish all the flaming arrows of the evil one. Take the helmet of salvation and the sword of the spirit, which is the word of God."
(Ephesians 6:16-17)

"And pray in the Spirit on all occasions with all kinds of prayers and requests. With this in mind, be alert and always keep on praying for all the world's people."
(Ephesians 6: 18-19)

"Peace to the brothers and sisters. And love with Faith from God the Father and the Lord Jesus Christ. Grace to all who love our Lord Jesus Christ with an undying love."
(Ephesians 6: 23-24

INTRODUCTION

Trouble eventually comes to everyone. Nobody escapes the daunting challenges of life. Spiritual warfare is also real. Spiritually induced attacks come from another dimension. They can be formidable and frightening. Evil exists. When unworldly forces attack us, human beings must have an extra layer of divine protection. Few souls are strong enough to stand alone against the full-blown threat posed by Satan's forces. As the Apostle Paul writes in Ephesians 6, "Our struggle is not against flesh and blood, but against the powers of this dark world and against the spiritual forces of evil in the heavenly realms." Therefore, Paul continues, "Put on the full armor of God, so that when the day of evil comes, you may be able to stand your ground." The Apostle understood that we are all susceptible to being blown away by the powers of darkness. In his letter to the early Christian churches in and around the city of Ephesus, Paul implores the faithful to prepare themselves for battle in the "full armor of God". The components of heavenly armor include:

the belt of truth; the breastplate of righteousness; our feet fitted with the readiness that comes from the gospel of peace; the shield of faith; the helmet of salvation and the sword of the Spirit, which is the word of God." The Apostle also advises us to "Pray on all occasions with prayers and requests." Hopefully, between God's armor and unceasing prayer, we can prevail against the principalities that dominate the material world. Even if you have not yet faced the wrath of pure evil, your time could be coming today, tomorrow or the day after that. Paul is seeking to prepare you for any degree of spiritual challenge. The Apostle serves as a worthy testimonial to withstanding evil. To say that he personally coped with many tribulations stands as a gross understatement. Paul faced vast and powerful opposition, including religious leaders and civil officials who tried to silence the "Good News" ministry of Jesus Christ. In the end, Paul surrendered his human life to proclaim and model that message. But the Apostle gave as good as he got. Without the courageous actions and words of the brilliant Paul, Christianity would not exist today. His visionary words of hope,

Introduction

peace, love, and service lit the Grand Torch that burns in the minds and hearts of 2.4 billion Christians throughout the world.

--Rev. Allen C. Liles

THE APOSTLE PAUL

If you had known Paul (or Saul) back in the day, his physical presence would not have captured your attention. He was a short man, between four and a half and five feet tall. He was also bald. A hooked nose dominated his pock-marked face. The Apostle walked in a bent over fashion that slowed his gait. It also made him seem even smaller. No one would describe Paul as striking or handsome. However, you would have become quickly aware of his intelligence and sense of purpose. Certain aspects of his intense and sometimes abrasive personality might have put you off. He could be prickly. The man loved to argue and give advice, usually unsolicited. Paul was a passionate advocate and/or defender of his point of view. If the Apostle felt strongly about anything, he made sure you knew about it—again, and then again. It must have felt like walking around with a contentious preacher in your pocket. Paul was not a comfortable person to just "hang with". He jangled many nerves. Things usually ended with him being verbally attacked, beaten, thrown into jail or run out of town. The scrappy little Apostle was passionate and directed by his inner guidance. His zealousness and single-minded determination to serve God and Jesus were two his greatest strengths. Paul's intellectual abilities were without peer. Although both a Roman and Greek citizen, The Apostle was born a Jew and treasured his Jewish heritage. He was a Pharisee and born an Israelite of the tribe of Benjamin. Israel's first king was Saul from the same tribe. In fact, Paul's Hebrew name was Saul (before his visit from Christ on the road to Damascus). But Paul was defined by much more than his citizenship. Without question, Paul was a remarkable thinker and wordsmith. Although not a dynamic speaker or physical presence, his way of framing words and ideas distinguished him from all others. His dedication to spreading Christianity affected world history, both then and now. Through his preaching and writings, Paul projected a wisdom and power that provided clarity to the ministry modeled by Jesus. As the Apostle traveled about encouraging (and sometimes admonishing) the early Christian churches, he also had to watch out for the "authorities". The Apostle was viewed by many as the ultimate troublemaker. Therein lay one of Paul's defining traits. He expressed his "Truth", regardless of whom it might offend. The little Apostle personified commitment and perseverance. He brought a giant intellect to the spiritual battlefield during a key time in religious history. In his letter to the Christian churches around Ephesus, Paul could speak with knowledge and credibility about "putting on the full armor of God". Standing strong against the Devil's schemes was his specialty. In his many travels, Paul was threatened, harassed, whipped, beaten with rods, run out of many towns, imprisoned, and finally martyred. He was shipwrecked three times. Through everything, he kept declaring the "good news" about His Lord Jesus Christ. Nothing discouraged or intimidated him. At the end, the tiny Apostle had fulfilled his spiritual destiny by spreading Christianity far and wide. Except for Jesus, no one person changed the religious and spiritual landscape more than Paul. His words still instruct and encourage us. This incomparable and literate man authored about half of the New Testament. This achievement originated from a person who began his religious and spiritual career persecuting Christians. The journey of Paul (formerly Saul the Persecutor) offers stunning proof God can indeed work miracles in anyone.

INNER PREPARATION FOR STUDY

OF EPHESIANS 6

Opening Prayer before beginning study of Ephesians 6:

LORD: I am prepared now to receive your Holy Word. I am open and receptive to putting on the Full Armor of God. Thank you for furnishing everything I need to protect myself against spiritual attacks and challenges that may come in my direction.

Relaxation—Find a quiet and comfortable place where you will not be disturbed. Sit with both of your feet flat on the floor. Place your hands gently in your lap with palms up. Now take a deep breath by inhaling through your nose. Hold your breath and count 1-2-3-4-5. Now open your mouth and slowly release your breath while counting 1-2-3-4-5-6-7-8. Now repeat the process two more times.

Concentration—Now visualize another person sitting directly across from you. It is the Apostle Paul. Focus on these words: "Thank you, Brother Paul, for instructing me on the lessons contained in Ephesians 6. I will do my best in learning how to defend myself from the powers that seek to undermine and compromise my soul. Thank you for the words and ideas that can help me stand against evil.

Realization—Feel your heart and soul being blessed by the Divine Presence of God. Become united with the Holy Spirit that lives inside of you. You are informed and supported by your inner spirit. Experience your mind, body and spirit being embraced and protected. You are a beloved Child of God, perfect in every way. God loves you. Please repeat two times: "God loves me." Remain in the silence for three full minutes.

Thanksgiving—Express your gratitude for this moment of spiritual preparation by saying three times "Thank you, God."

NIV BIBLE TEXT

Verse 1······Children, obey your parents in the Lord, for this is right.

2····"Honor your father and mother" which is the first commandment with a promise—

3···so that it may go well with you and that you may enjoy long life on the earth."

4···Fathers, do not exasperate your children, instead bring them up in the training and instruction of the Lord.

5···Slaves, obey your earthly masters with respect and fear, and with sincerity of the heart, just as you would obey Christ.

6···Obey them not only to win their favor when their eye is on you, but as slaves of Christ, doing the will of God from your heart.

7···Serve wholeheartedly, as if you were serving the Lord, not people,

8···because you know that the Lord will reward each one for whatever good they do, whether they are slave or free.

9···And masters, treat your slaves in the same way. Do not threaten them, since you that he who is both their Master and yours is in heaven, and there is no favoritism with him.

10···Finally be strong in the Lord and in his mighty power.

11—Put on the full armor of God, so that you can take your stand against the devil's schemes.

12—For our struggle is not against flesh and blood, but against the rulers, against the authorities, against the powers of this dark world and against the spiritual forces of evil in the heavenly realms.

13—Therefore put on the full armor of God so when the day of evil comes, you may be able to stand your ground, and after you have done everything, to stand.

14—Stand firm then, with the belt of truth buckled around your waist, with the breastplate of righteousness in place,

15—and your feet fitted with the readiness that comes from the gospel of peace.

16—In addition to all this, take up the shield of faith with which you can extinguish all the flaming arrows of the evil one.

17—Take the helmet of salvation and the sword of the Spirit, which is the word of God.

18—And pray in the Spirit on all occasions with all kinds of prayers and requests. With this in mind, be alert and always keep on praying for all the word's people.

19—Pray also for me, that whenever I speak, words may be given me so that I will fearlessly make known the mystery of the gospel,

20—for which I am an ambassador in chains. Pray that I might declare it fearlessly, as I should.

21—Tychicus, the dear brother and faithful servant of the Lord, will tell you everything, so that you also know how I am and what I am doing.

22—I am sending him to you for this very purpose so that you may know how we are and that he may encourage you.

23--Peace to the brothers and sisters and love with faith from God the Father and the Lord Jesus Christ.

24—Grace to all who love our Lord Jesus Christ with an undying love."

TEXT COMMENTARY

EPHESIANS 6: 1-3—INSTRUCTIONS TO CHILDREN

Ephesians 1: 1—Children, obey your parents in the Lord, for this is right.

Ephesians 1: 2—"Honor your father and mother" which is the first commandment with a promise—

Ephesians 1: 3—so that it may go well with you and that you may en- joy long life on the earth."

EPHESIANS 6:4—INSTRUCTIONS TO PARENTS

Ephesians 1:4—"Fathers, do not exasperate your children; instead, bring them up in the training and instruction of the Lord."

The Apostle Paul devoted his life trying to encourage correct actions and respectful behavior. When instructing the early Christians, he urged them to act in a Christ-like manner. That included urging children to obey their parents, and parents not to frustrate their children. Paul was most at home when directing others. On more than one occasion, some of those he instructed did not want or appreciate his advice. Paul was dealing with an almost impossible task: trying to change or alter human nature. Children often do not want to obey their parents. In fact, many younger people wait for their parent's directions so they can do the exact opposite. Paul must have understood that aspect of parent-child relationships. Still, his words are clear in telling children to obey and honor their parents. It is, Paul reminds us, one of the 10 Commandments. To sweeten the pot for children, he offers an incentive. He tells the young ones that being obedient and respectful to their parents will help things go well for them in their lives. It could even contribute to their longevity. Of course, most young people are not focusing on living longer lives at this point. The Apostle had no doubt that treating parents well would bring bounteous blessings to both sides. Paul wanted children to understand and accept the personal benefits of obeying and honoring their parents. Why would he want to make this effort? First, obeying and practicing an official Commandment is always a good thing in God's eyes. Secondly, Paul may have observed the pain that comes to parents when children ignore their advice or demands. When Paul perceived any wrong, it was his nature to set things straight. Without question, the committed Apostle needed considerable strength and faith to endure constant rejection from both individuals and institutions. In this passage from scripture, Paul tried to invoke God's Holy name as a reward for doing the right thing. However, in many parent-child relationships, even receiving approval from God might not be enough to shift behaviors. In his warning to "Fathers" not to exasperate their children, Paul seems to understand that parents can create problems for their children through unrealistic expectations and overbearing direction. In his exhortations to both sides, the Apostle Paul hoped to build more constructive and respectful family relationships.

EPHESIANS 6: 5
Instructions To
Slaves And Masters

EPHESIANS 6: 5—"Slaves, obey your earthly masters with respect and fear; and with sincerity of heart, just as you would obey Christ.

EPHESIANS 6:6 –Obey them to not only win their favor when their eye is on you, but as slaves of Christ, doing the will of God from your heart.

EPHESIANS 6:7—Serve wholeheartedly, as if you were serving the Lord, not people,

EPHESIANS 6:8—because you know the Lord will reward each one for whatever good they do, whether they are slave or free.

EPHESIANS 6:9—And masters, treat your slaves in the same way. Do not threaten them, since you know that he who is both their master and yours in heaven, and there is no favoritism with him.

∞

Ephesians 6

So why does the Apostle Paul feel it necessary to take on the relationship between slaves and masters? In some ways, it continues his practice of dispensing advice to one and all. In the preceding chapter (Ephesians 5) he focused on the marital responsibilities between husbands and wives. The Apostle urged the husband to treat his wife as "holy" and to see her as a "radiant church". He told the wife to "submit yourself to your husband as you would would to the Lord". Paul also invoked a comparison to Christ acting as the head of the church and concerned about all relationships. At the beginning of Ephesians 6, Paul continues his exhortations regarding family dynamics. He specifically addresses the interactions between parents and children. The Apostle is concerned about the potential for family conflicts. In evaluating Paul's approach to ministry, he sees himself as the consummate "fixer" of human relationships. That also extends to congregants within a church body. However, his exhortations to "masters and slaves" seems idealistic. Yet, the dedicated Apostle seems willing to take it on the problem. In his writings, one can sense Paul's frustrations with not only battling Satan, but also human nature. However, his instructions to slaves and their masters may ignore reality. Free will choice is absent from the relationship between masters and slaves. Husbands and wives choose each other. Congregants can stay or go from their individual churches. But slaves possess no such freedom. So why would Paul jump in and attempt to "fix" an already strained relationship? Yet perhaps more curiously, why did he think slave masters would even care about his opinion? Reading between the lines, the Apostle may have been aware of trouble between the slaves and their masters in Ephesus. Since his specialty was sorting out people problems, this could have been an attempt to healing relations in general. As Paul had tried other times, he sought to frame behaviors between masters and slaves as somehow akin to both seeking favor from God. The Apostle could be persuasive when he invoked the name of God to accomplish his objectives. But improving relationships between masters and slaves? That seems problematic at best. However, Paul's inherent nature of wanting to reconcile all parties may have inspired him to make the attempt. The Apostle never backed away from expressing an unpopular opinion, no matter who was involved. He always exhibited tenacity and determination, even though it made him susceptible to spiritual attacks.

EPHESIANS 6:10 - 11
Put On The Full Armor Of God

Ephesians 6:10—Finally, be strong in the Lord and in his mighty power.

Ephesians 6:11—Put on the full armor of God, so that you can take your stand against the devil's schemes.

These two verses begin Paul's famous passage about "Putting on the Full Armor of God." This was a defensive action the Apostle must have practiced countless times. His ministry on behalf of Christianity produced personal trouble for Paul wherever he went. However, in the Apostle's mind, his spiritual direction from God and Jesus could not be clearer. He was to spread "The Good News" among the Gentiles. Despite hardships, threats or intimidation, Paul soldiered on. He traveled through many countries and areas, planting seeds of encouragement and support for the various churches. Yet, Paul encountered many who did not want to hear about this radical new teaching. In fact, most state officials (and many religious leaders) were aligned against anyone promoting a different way of theological thinking. The Apostle and his Christian followers were threatened, hassled, beaten with rods, stoned, and often tossed into the closest prison. He was often run out of town with a howling mob close behind him. One can visualize the faithful Paul suiting up in God's armor to deflect the flaming arrows of criticism, ridicule, and physical harm. He understood that being God's servant required an extra measure of spiritual strength. Taking a stand against the "devil's schemes" was dangerous. Human attacks were bad enough. However, the dark side was more cunning and baffling. It could be both subtle and direct in launching assaults. Pure evil often came at its victims with well-disguised guile. Of course, the Principalities are aware of our many human weaknesses. If we are obsessed with money, power, fame, or any material desire, they already know about it. The spiritual assault comes designed to attack these most vulnerable shortcomings. In these two verses, Paul offers God's "Full Armor" as protection. He states that being clad in God's armor can help us withstand any storm. Often, when we are under attack by spiritual

Ephesians 6: 10 - 11

forces, there is a feeling of being blown away. Being able to "stand" against the powers of evil should remain our #1 spiritual goal. In these verses, The Apostle offers the "Full Armor of God" to help protect us.

EPHESIANS 6:12
Who We Struggle Against

"For our struggle is not against flesh and blood, but against the rulers, against the authorities, against the powers of this dark world and against the spiritual forces of evil in the heavenly realms."

In this verse, Paul gives a fuller explanation of the type forces aligned against us. He wants to make sure we understand that spiritual assaults are different from life's usual challenges. These attacks are thoughtful, premeditated and carefully planned. Confrontations that involve our souls are drawn and carried out with deadly precision. Meticulous effort goes into knocking us off kilter spiritually. In many cases, the goal is not just to destabilize or confuse us. If the dark side sees our God-potential as a legitimate threat, complete destruction might be required. At these times, you and I need powerful resources to defend and protect us. The forces of evil can upend and defeat the strongest human being. Most people tend to downplay threats that remain invisible to the five senses. If we cannot see, hear, feel, taste or smell the danger, we may disregard it. The existential threat to our safety may arrive in many attractive forms. Outer beauty, an opportunity for wealth and status or access to power are potent temptations. Never underestimate the principalities of evil, Paul reminds us. We must stay forever on the alert. The Apostle warns that we are not struggling against flesh and blood. These threats come from another universe. We may find ourselves in the jaws of our attackers long before they ever start devouring us. These dark powers descend toward us from the "heavenly realms". We should never dismiss their otherworldly capabilities. Only The Full Armor of God can deliver us from evil. It is interesting that this heavenly protection only includes frontal armor. Evidently, Paul never considered any armor for our backsides. He could not envision us turning tail and running away from evil. Paul saw God's brave warriors always pressing forward to victory in the battle for souls.

EPHESIANS 6:13
Standing Our Ground Against Evil

"Therefore put on the full armor of God, so that when the day of evil comes, you may be able to stand your ground, and after you have done everything, to stand."

Paul predicts that the "day of evil" will come for everyone. There are just too many temptations and traps on the human scene for us to escape unscathed. No one stays trouble free forever. "Evil" arrived many times for The Apostle and his band of cohorts. As this Roman and Greek scholar traveled the world promoting Christianity, problems awaited him almost everywhere. We must marvel at the courage Paul displayed as he pressed on with his sacred mission. Even some of the churches The Apostle sought to form and encourage were not always welcoming. In Paul's mind, he was only there to help. However, for many church leaders and congregants, his lecturing and admonitions sometimes proved irritating. For them, he was the "outside consultant" from the home office sent to judge and reorganize them. Probably more than a few church leaders were happy when his chariot disappeared over the horizon. Yet, his eloquent and timeless words were filled with wisdom and power. Reading his inspiring rhetoric, we can only be grateful for his soaring faith in God, Jesus, and his dedicated efforts in spreading Christianity to the Gentiles. The Apostle's uplifting words resonate today. He possessed uncommon courage and dedication. He sometimes had to overcome his own "followers" aligned against him. That must have felt especially disheartening. In that sense, the Apostle faced the exact same treatment experienced by Jesus during his own troubled ministry. Even today, a certain percentage of minds remain hostile to Christianity. Followers of Jesus still face persecution throughout the world. Great dangers abound for those who embrace the Jesus teachings. Christians must keep their "Full Armor of God" close at hand, ready for any spiritual threat.

EPHESIANS 6:14
The Belt Of Truth And Breastplate Of Righteousness

"Stand firm then, with the belt of truth buckled around your waist, with the breastplate of righteousness in place."

Spiritual Truth represents a basic component of God's full armor. Falsehoods and lies litter the world's landscape. God's Truth is eternal and unchanging. Inner wisdom remains the same today, tomorrow and forever. You can redeem Heaven's promissory notes anytime and anywhere. The material world vacillates and shifts. It can be approving of you one day and castigating you the next. Truth is all-encompassing and forever relevant. Meanwhile, the "principalities of darkness" specialize in lies, confusion and chaos. Whenever a sacred blast of Truth (with a capital "T") arrives, it brings clarity. Evil must then retreat and scatter. Dark always flees from the Light. They are natural enemies. Truth cannot be hidden or diffused. It does not practice denial or deception. The first place we must seek Truth is within ourselves. There we find the Holy Spirit. It serves as our comforter and guide. Real and unvarnished Truth always prevails at center of our being. God placed the Holy Spirit within us during the Creation process. It never leads us astray. In the 12 Step Recovery programs we are encouraged to become honest about our own human shortcomings. The 4th step instructs us to make a "searching and fearless inventory of ourselves". Buckling the "Belt of Truth" around our waist means we have accepted the unvarnished Truth about ourselves. The "Breastplate of Righteousness" also equips us to deflect the devil's "flaming arrows". Being human and vulnerable, we can get knocked off course by a spiritual confrontation. The "Breastplate" provides protection against the dark forces that seek our soul destruction. As the Apostle Paul visited churches and congregants to instruct them on "righteous" conduct, he had to dodge negative words and physical threats. As we face our own challenges, it helps to have a sturdy breastplate of to protect us from emotional and physical dangers. As human beings, we need God's armor to survive.

EPHESIANS 6:15
Our Feet Fitted With Readiness
From The Gospel of Peace

"And with your feet fitted with the readiness that comes from the gospel of peace."

In Paul's letters to the new churches, there was an underlying theme of asking the followers of Jesus to become better prepared for spiritual service. That probably meant that the Apostle viewed these early Christians as being in a state of unreadiness. In fact, most human beings are not ready when trouble strikes. We can live our lives in complete denial about negative situations. Complacency entices almost everyone. Denying the truth is easy. Confronting that denial requires awareness, acceptance and action ("The 3 A's"). No sane person enjoys confrontation. Most of us try to "get along". Recognizing our own shortcomings is especially uncomfortable. Paul is warning the early churches about the realities of a

Christian life. They are being called to serve Christ. They must also deal with the human tendencies toward procrastination, laziness, and an aversion to confrontation. Human nature is still the same now as in Paul's day. All of us would prefer to move along without facing emotional storms that upset the status quo. But Paul warns us about the dangers of spiritual warfare. He wants us to know about the Full Armor of God. Part of that sacred armor is fitting our feet with the Gospel of Peace. In combat of any kind, we must stay ready to move fast. How do we accomplish that? The Gospel of Peace includes some excellent resources. You and I can turn to the inspirational words contained in the Holy Bible. Reading the Word of God daily helps us prepare for speedy action when trouble arrives. Prayer and meditation are other proven methods of becoming ready for anything. We must always keep our feet firmly planted on Holy Ground. When aligned in Oneness with God, we cannot be blown away by evil winds. Spiritual tornadoes can tear through anybody's life without warning. Focusing on the eternal Truths of God keeps us fitted for speed. A quick response to danger could save the day.

EPHESIANS 6:16
The Shield of Faith

"In addition to all this, take up the shield of faith, with which you can extinguish all the flaming arrows of the evil one."

Keeping the faith during a spiritual attack can be hard. But no alternative is stronger than "faith" when the flaming arrows begin to fly. Of course, we can always choose to rely on our own resources rather seek outside spiritual help. We might even consider trusting other human beings or institutions. We could always give up and surrender without a fight. There is also the option of going into hiding and praying that the other side never finds us. Most people facing off against evil would probably prefer a non-confrontational approach. However, if we do decide to fight the dark side, God's "Shield of Faith" could make the difference. Flaming arrows can scream at us from many directions. The Apostle Paul dealt with countless such "arrows", including being shipwrecked, beaten and imprisoned. Without possessing a sturdy Shield of Faith, he might not have survived. What are the basic materials that make up the eternal shield? Faith itself serves as the key component. Hebrews 11: 1 defines faith as "Having confidence in what we hope for and assurance about what we do not see." That means putting our trust in the invisible. Challenges can arrive 24/7 without warning. When the dry winds of testing arrive, we must immediately fetch our shield of faith. Never hesitate. Lift this powerful Heaven-made protective gear in front of you. Turn away any weapons that seek your destruction. Trust God. Believe that His Armor will sustain you. The Apostle Paul wants all of God's servants to have the best defenses available. The Shield of Faith acts as the primary element in your spiritual tool kit. Keep it handy so that you can live to fight another day.

EPHESIANS 6:17
The Helmet of Salvation and Sword of The Spirit

"Take the helmet of salvation and the sword of the spirit, which is the word of God."

"Salvation" is defined as "the state of being protected or saved from harm." The spiritual meaning could be expanded to include the "saving of a soul". That would seem to apply in much of Paul's Ephesians 6 writing. In spiritual warfare, the goal of evil is clear: it wants to either assume control or outright destroy our soul. Capturing or killing our spiritual essence removes us from the battlefield. Satan then has one less human soul to worry about. The principalities of darkness want to confuse and corrupt our brains. It starts with trying to deceive the human mind. If our thinking can be turned toward evil, defeating the entire soul becomes a much simpler task. In this important verse, Paul urges us to employ the "sword of the spirit, which is the "word of God." That means you and I can find hope and support in the pages of the Holy Bible. God uses the

Ephesians 6

"Good Book" to provide spiritual ammunition in any battle against evil. From the Psalms in the Old Testament to the words of Jesus and the writings of Paul in the New Testament, the Bible teems with wisdom and inspiration. Shielding our brains with eternal teachings can turn away the scariest assault. The "helmet of salvation" is an extra protection for our vulnerable minds. Unless our thinking stays straight, Satan could lead us into temptation and defeat. During a spiritual attack, only perfect clarity can bring us victory over evil.

EPHESIANS 6:18
Praying In The Spirit

"And pray in the Spirit on all occasions with all kinds of prayers and requests. With this in mind, be alert and always keep on praying for all of the Lord's people."

Prayer is a crucial part of surviving any spiritual attack. Staying in a prayerful state improves our chances of coping with assaults on our soul. When Paul wrote about "praying on all occasions", he is saying that God wants us to stay plugged into the Divine. The Apostle says we must always maintain a sacred connection with God and Jesus. However, unless prayer is already an established habit, most people only pray when something happens that requires immediate attention. Paul recommends that we "pray without ceasing." He assures us that God considers every prayer, no matter how insignificant it might seem. Directing us to pray "on all occasions and with all kinds of prayers," Paul suggests that no prayer is too small to get God's attention. In fact, by urging us to "stay alert", Spirit is asking that we constantly scan our immediate environment for any prayer needs that might be lurking nearby. We should never exclude anyone or anything that could benefit from our prayers. Without question, prayer ranks as our best act of personal involvement with God. The Apostle always searched for ways to bless others through prayer. Encouraging human beings to pray for each other provides an opportunity to practice the Golden Rule. "Praying in the Spirit" can also be a good way of bringing the faithful together in unity. In telling us to be "alert" for prayer possibilities, Paul implores all Christians to stay connected with each other. Building a common bond can help a community of believers to grow and expand. Paul never missed a chance to remind everyone about the importance of prayer. Even in his most dire days, the Apostle never quit praying.

EPHESIANS 6: 19 - 20
Pray For The Ambassador In Chains

"Pray also for me, that whenever I speak, words may be given me that so that I will fearlessly make known the mystery of the gospel,

Ephesians 6:20-- for which I am an ambassador in chains. Pray that I may declare it fearlessly as I should."

One feels great empathy for the beleaguered Apostle. Paul had taken on the burden of spreading the gospel of Jesus Christ. In return for his sacred commitment to serve God and Jesus, he received non-stop spiritual attacks. How many of us could hold up under such unceasing physical, mental, and spiritual torture? Yet, Paul continued to persevere and serve. He admits to seeking as much prayer support as possible. The Apostle uses the word "fearlessly" in each of these two verses. Without question, fear can become a constant companion when spiritual assaults overwhelm us. Referring to himself as "an ambassador in chains", the Apostle also reminds others of his imprisonment. You can almost hear Paul stating (with pride): "Look at what I am willing to endure on God's behalf". He could have been justified in adding "So, what are you complaining about?" Throughout his service to God and Jesus, the Apostle displayed extraordinary courage, unrelenting determination, and tireless stamina in pursuing his Holy mission. Paul earned his status as the most important person in the New Testament, outside of Jesus Christ himself.

EPHESIANS 6: 21 - 24
Encouragement, Peace, Love, Faith
And Grace To All Who Love Jesus

Ephesians 6: 21— Tychicus, the dear brother and faithful servant in the Lord, will tell you everything, so you may also ask how I am and what I am doing.

Ephesians 6:22—I am sending him to you for this very purpose, that you may know how we are, and that he may encourage you.

Ephesians 6: 23—Peace to the brothers and sisters, and love with faith from God the Father and the Lord Jesus Christ.

Ephesians 6:24—Grace to all who love our Lord Jesus Christ with an undying love.

Paul was a communicator who attempted to promote collegial and professional relations with the churches he served. But he first remained a warrior for God and Jesus, no matter what might be happening in his life.

Ephesians 6

The Apostle's determination to spread Christianity among the Gentiles was amazing. Despite powerful opposition that would have defeated anyone else, he remained steadfast and determined. In these verses, Paul continued to assure others that God and Jesus sent their love and faith. He also wanted to keep everyone posted on his progress, as well as the problems. Without question, the Apostle understood the realities and dangers of his mission. Being the leader of an unpopular new religious doctrine would test anyone's faith. His spiritual assignment demanded that Paul be unyielding. Using the word "undying" in verse 24 underlines his dedication and commitment. The Apostle serves as a role model as we endure our own spiritual attacks. He urges us stand and fight against evil. He assures us that we need not battle Satan alone. Without this extra spiritual protection, we might be in danger of losing our soul. You can almost hear the Apostle encouraging us to keep practicing our faith. Paul wants every Christian soldier to keep marching onward and upward to victory. This brave and undaunted warrior stands as an incomparable example of unwavering determina-

Ephesians 6: 21 - 24

tion. Do you and I have the courage to survive a spiritual attack? Yes, I believe we do. Clad in the Full Armor of God, we can be victors for Christ.

OTHER IMPORTANT VERSES IN PAUL'S LETTER TO THE EPHESIANS

EPHESIANS 1: 8-9—"With all wisdom and understanding, he made known to us the mystery of his will, to be put into effect when the times reach their fulfillment—to bring unity to all things on heaven and earth."

EPHESIANS 1: 13—"And you were also included with Christ when you heard the message of truth, the gospel of your salvation. When you believed, he marked you with a seal-- the Holy Spirit."

EPHESIANS 1:18—"I pray that the eyes of your heart may be enlightened in order that you may know the hope to which he has called you."

EPHESIANS 2: 8—"It is by grace that you have been saved. It is the gift of God, not by works, so that no one may boast. But we are God's handiwork, created in Jesus Christ to do good works."

EPHESIANS 2: 14—"For he himself is our peace. He made both Jews and Gentiles. He destroyed the barrier between them, the dividing wall of hostility."

EPHESIANS 2: 21—"In Jesus, the whole building is joined and rises to become a Holy Temple. In him, you are now being built together."

EPHESIANS 3:6—"The Gentiles are heirs with Israel and sharers together in the promise of Jesus Christ."

EPHESIANS 3:17—"And I pray that you, being established in love, will grasp how long and high and deep is the love of Christ."

EPHESIANS 4:1-3—"As a prisoner for the Lord, I urge you to live a life worthy of the calling you have received. Be completely humble and patient with one another in Love. Make every effort to stay in unity of the spirit through the bond of peace. Put off falsehoods and speak truthfully to your neighbor Do not let the sun go down while you are still angry."

Other Important Verses In Paul's Letter To The Ephesians

EPHESIANS 5:1-2—"May we follow God's example and act as dearly loved children, by walking in the ways of love. Just as Christ loved us and gave himself up for us, may we also offer a fragrant sacrifice to God."

EPHESIANS 5: 8-9—"For you were once in darkness but now you are a light for God. Live as children of the Light. The fruit of the Light consists of goodness, righteousness and truth."

EPHESIANS 5: 13—"Be careful then how you live—not as unwise but wise. Make the most of every opportunity."

EPHESIANS 5: 19—"Sing and make music from your heart. Give thought for everything in the name of our Lord Jesus Christ."

WHAT ABOUT EPHESUS?

Ephesus was an ancient Greek city (now located in western Turkey) adjacent to the Aegean Sea. It was founded in 10th century BC on the coast of Ionia. During the Classic Greek Age, it was one of the 12 cities of the Ionic League.

The city was famous for the nearby Temple of Artemis, completed in 550 BC, which was deemed one of the Seven Wonders of the ancient world. Artemis was a famous Greek Goddess of wild animals and the wilderness. Ephesus itself was destroyed by the Goths in 263. It was rebuilt and then partially destroyed again by an earthquake in AD 614. It now lies underneath an area near the city of Selcuk in Izmir Province in western Turkey.

Ephesus was one of the seven churches of Asia that are cited in the Book of Revelation. The Gospel of John may have been written in Ephesus. The city also served as the site of several 5th century Christian Councils.

The importance of Ephesus as a commercial center declined as its harbor was slowly silted up by a nearby river despite repeated dredging during the city's history. The loss of its harbor caused Ephesus to lose its access to the Aegean Sea, which was important for trade. People soon began leaving the lowland of the city for the surrounding hills. The ruins of the temples were used as building blocks for new homes. Marble sculptures were ground to powder to make lime for plaster. Sackings by the Arabs in the years 654-655 hastened the city's decline even further. Crusaders passing through the region in the 1300s were surprised to find only a small village. Ephesus was completely abandoned by the 15th century.

However, it was an important city for early Christianity in the AD 50's. The Apostle Paul lived in Ephesus from AD 52-54. He spent his time working with the local Christian and Jewish congregations and organizing missionary activities in nearby areas. He attended the Jewish synagogue in Ephesus for a time. However, The Apostle met with resistance from many in the local congregations. He eventually formed a community of Jewish Christians. A silversmith named Demetrios stirred up a mob against Paul, saying that he was endangering the liveli-

What About Ephesus?

hood of those who were making shrines to the goddess Artemis. Paul wrote the first letter to the Corinthians, possibly from a prison tower, while in Ephesus. He wrote the Letter to the Ephesians while he was imprisoned in Rome around 62 AD.

Roman Asia also has been associated with John, one of Jesus' original apostles. It is believed that John wrote the New Testament book bearing his name while in Ephesus 90-100 AD. A local legend also claimed that the Virgin Mary may have spent her last years in Ephesus. The Church of Mary, near the old harbor, was the setting for the Third Ecumenical Council in 431. A Second Council of Ephesus occurred in 449, but its controversial acts were never approved by the Catholics.

The original site of Ephesus is now one of the largest archaeological sites in the Eastern Mediterranean. The digging continues yet today.

GOD VISITS PAUL IN PRISON

BREAKING NEWS

FOR IMMEDIATE RELEASE:

ROME—God visited The Apostle Paul in his prison cell in Rome today. The Creator and Ruler of the Universe arrived unannounced at High Noon. He was unaccompanied, although the Archangel Michael was spotted outside the prison. The major angel was leaning against a nearby building, where he remained while God was inside the well-fortified jail.

According to a guard who witnessed the Holy visit, a surprised Paul rose to greet God with outstretched arms. They embraced for several minutes. The Apostle wept as the Creator of the Universe held him close.

"Oh, my Father!", I have missed you so much," Paul was heard to say.

"My son, I have always been near you," God replied. "Have you not felt My divine Presence? I AM nearer than your hands or feet."

Ephesians 6

"I'm sure that's true," the little Apostle replied, "But it can really get lonesome sometimes, especially here in prison. The authorities will not allow me to have any regular visitors. They say I am a bad influence."

"I've always thought of you as the best possible influence," God reportedly said.

"Oh, I hope that is true," Paul laughed. "I can be such a nag sometimes. It's just my nature, I guess."

God smiled and invited Paul to sit. The Apostle reclined on his prison bunk while a makeshift chair suddenly materialized for the Creator.

"I AM here for two reasons," God said, "First, I have brought you a fresh supply of My Armor. Paul, you have been through so many spiritual attacks. Your Shield of Faith is dented in several places. I notice that your original Belt of Truth has become frayed. I also see your Breastplate of Righteousness has become badly tarnished and needs polishing. I believe you could use some new, more stylish shoes. These hip new designers have done great things with spiritual footwear these days. By the way, your Sword of the Spirit looks old and dull. I doubt if it could cut through soft butter. My dear boy, you simply need a wardrobe renovation. I will be glad to supply you."

"I appreciate that," Paul acknowledged, "I know you are right. It is funny that you would mention my Full Armor. I am just finishing up the Epistle to the Ephesians. Your sacred Armor is a big part of my imagery and message."

"Human beings need extra protection from spiritual attacks now more than ever," God acknowledged. "So many people want to confront true evil without any help. That can be a huge mistake. It puts everybody at risk. Of course, the dark side loves it when people try to fight them off alone. Human beings are just no match for the evil-doers without My help."

"I know that spiritual attacks are real," Paul told God. "Look at me. I am more bent over than usual because the constant battering. That old "thorn in my flesh" has been tearing at me day and night."

Ephesians 6

The prison guard reported there was a brief silence between God and Paul. Then, Spirit placed His hand on the Apostle's shoulder and told him: "About that "thorn", My son, you will soon leave it behind."

"What do you mean, Father?" Paul asked.

"I said I came here for two reasons," Spirit continued. "I am calling you back to Heaven soon. You will be martyred within the next few weeks."

According to the guard, Paul emitted a cry. However, the jailer noted, it was hard to identify the exact nature of the emotion. At first, he thought it sounded mournful. However, Paul soon began smiling. His mood seemed to change into something more positive.

"The crazy little Apostle seemed almost giddy." The guard said, "I was surprised."

"Oh, thank you," Paul told God. "I talked about this paradox in my letter to the Philippians when I wrote "To live is Christ and to die is gain." I was torn then about which way to go. Now, I am glad everything is settled. Of course, dying a violent death will not be easy. However, when that time comes, I will still be clad in your Full Armor. Until then, I will keep proclaiming the Truth about you and Jesus. Yet it is true. I am looking forward to being in Heaven for eternity."

The prison guard said God embraced Paul one final time before disappearing through the bars of the cell.

"Jesus and I will be there to welcome you home," Spirit told the Apostle. "I will say to you: "Well done, My good and faithful servant. You are My beloved child. in whom I AM well pleased."

The Roman jailer said Paul drifted off to sleep in his cell after God departed. He was smiling.

A FANTASY OF PAUL'S THOUGHTS BEFORE MARTYRDOM

This is my fantasy account of The Apostle Paul's final thoughts on the night before his martyrdom in May, A.D. 68. The Roman Emperor Nero, who ordered Paul's execution, would himself be dead by suicide less than a month later.

"To all My friends and followers in Christ. I bring you Greetings. The time for me has finally arrived. My personal jailer, dear friend that he has become, shared the news less than an hour ago. The crazy Nero has finally acted. My fate is sealed. Evidently, I will be transported at dawn to an obscure place south of the city, far removed from the prison itself. There were will no opportunity for any of my followers to witness the final moments. I recall the sordid stories about the public humiliation suffered by our brother Jesus Christ during his public Crucifixion. In that instance, the authorities wanted people to witness His suffering. They hoped it might serve as a warning to any more would-be messiahs. That did not

work out so well for them, especially when Jesus emerged from the tomb three days later. Evil has a way of expecting success and then experiencing conspicuous failure. I honestly wonder what Nero expects to realize from quietly killing me. Who knows? The poor devil is such a fruitless man. Since the terrible fire here in Rome three years ago, the fool has become even more unhinged. He exacted some terrible retribution from my fellow Christians, burning many of them at the stake. I am not sure how he missed killing me during that purge. I did try to lie low while the carnage was happening. What a deranged and evil young man. Imagine his idiotic fiddling while the city burned during the fire! History will not be kind to such a human failure, nor should it be. I believe most historians will dismiss Nero as an addled degenerate. The young Emperor never had the courage to even meet with me. My jailer told me there was a rumor he was deathly afraid of my "spiritual powers". According to the story making the rounds, Nero was worried I might put a spell on him. He disrespected a son of Rome by never granting me an audience, but that hardly bears mentioning. If we had met, what would I have said to him? That God forgives him?

Although I believe the Father forgives all sinners, I am not sure a complete idiot like Nero would have understood what I was telling him. I pity all people, especially the great and powerful, who have no interest in knowing about Jesus or the fruits of the spirit. Oh, what they are missing! I remember asking God what happens to souls like Nero when they enter Heaven. The Father reaffirmed that no human soul is ever denied admission to the Kingdom. But He also told me that the biggest sinners cannot avoid some personal accountability for their earthly actions. For example, they must spend eons in spiritual instruction and repentance before receiving even minor heavenly responsibilities. Who knows if that is true? I guess I will learn that and many other things soon. How do I feel about my time on earth coming to an end? I recall writing to the church at Philippi, "For to me, to live is Christ and to die is gain." I believe that. I have been so honored to serve the Lord. Yet I must admit the idea of spending eternity in close approximation to both God and Jesus seems quite attractive. I am also looking forward to watching the progress of Christianity unfold. I am sure it will be a challenging, interesting, and uneven jour-

ney. *I found the resistance to The Good News extraordinary. I have Jewish inclinations, but the Jews have been among my most intractable opponents. They certainly had mixed feelings about Jesus when He was alive. In one sense, He was their long-awaited Messiah. In another, they could not wait to crucify Him. The High Priest Caiaphas was the one who wanted the troublemaker gone. Pilate probably would have released Jesus, but the priests saw an opportunity to silence Him forever. In general, the Jewish establishment was never happy with me either. To them, I was a pain in the backside. However, I never really cared about what they thought. I knew who I was. I understood my spiritual assignment, which was to spread the Good News among the Gentiles. It was Peter's job to work the Jewish side of the map. However, I still could not avoid getting in trouble with every Jewish leader I encountered. Oh, how they hated my various letters to the new Christian churches! They especially disliked the one to the Ephesians. Describing how church goers should put on the "whole armor of God" threatened them to no end. The idea of armed resistance worried them. The Jewish leaders were never pleased with Christianity in general. Of course, they had Jesus' blood on their hands. With all due respect, the Jews are so tradition bound. It did not help that my disregard of the Torah was an open secret. I have never been tactful about hiding my feelings about anything. My best friends were tolerant of me, but I know they saw me as rigid and unyielding. They would say to me "Paul, why don't you use some tact?" or could you just "lighten up a little"? They were right, I guess. But that was never my nature. If I had been more submissive, I probably could have avoided all that jail time. But I just never thought about wasting my precious time on fools and numbskulls. That includes the nay-sayers and malcontents at the various churches. Yes, I had a hard life in many ways. Still, I never once thought about giving up my sacred assignment. Well, wait a minute. I must be honest. After a couple of shipwrecks and a few of the beatings, I did think about seeking some relief. But God needed what I had to offer, so I kept going. I thank Him for "The Full Armor". It saved me more than once. When all is said and done, serving God and Jesus has been the blessing of my life. It all began when I was blinded on the road to Damascus. After my sight came back, I knew what I had to do. For more than 30 years now, I have done everything God and Jesus asked of me. When I go to be with them tomorrow, my human story will end. But my eternal journey will just be commencing. I hope the many letters I wrote to the various churches will survive my passing. They represent some of my best work. I heard God thought they were quite helpful for the congregants. Anyway, that is what Jesus told me.*

A FANTASY OF NERO'S THOUGHTS

Fantasy Thoughts From The Roman Emperor Nero On The Night Before The Apostle Paul's Martyrdom:

Tomorrow I will finally be rid of that religious pest known as "Paul The Epistle" or "Apostle". I always forget which, but forgetfulness may be the least of my problems these days. I am losing what may be left of my feeble mind. I see enemies everywhere. It all began when they insisted that I become Emperor at the age of sixteen. My crazy mother Agrippa kept nagging me until I agreed to do it. What a big-time mistake! I never forgave her. Truth be told, that may have been the real reason I had her murdered. I was not ready for the responsibility that comes with being the Emperor of a nation like Rome. I tried to be a man of the people. The poorer souls liked me. But official Rome? They all hated my guts. I am sure I gave them ample reasons to detest me. Was I irresponsible? Absolutely! Did I drink too much? There was no doubt about it. In fact, I was drunk most of the time.

That is how I kept sane. Did I chase women every waking hour of the day or night? I plead guilty as charged. Was I a terrible administrator? I could not administer my way out of a paper bag, even if I tried. In a word, I was an abject failure at being an Emperor of the great Roman Empire. Do you think that being so inept did not bother me? Yes, of course it did. Then when "The Fire" happened, I was really exposed and ridiculed for my shortcomings. The story about me fiddling while Rome burned was true. Of course, I was drunk as a skunk at the time. Anyway, I tried to shift the blame to those clueless Christians. I fed them to the Lions, burned them at the stake, threw them off cliffs and made their lives miserable. Now, tomorrow, I will finally be rid of their bothersome leader. The old man should not be worried. He will probably be headed for Heaven and a fancy banquet with God and his precious Jesus. I am planning to follow him in a couple of weeks via suicide (if I can find the courage). However, something tells me that I may be traveling in the opposite direction from the Epistle. I doubt anyone will throw a good old-fashioned Roman orgy in my honor when I depart for purgatory. However, I plan to take my fiddle and a jug of wine with me. At least I can make my own music and have a few laughs while I burn in hell."

THE TWELVE GIFTS OF EPHESIANS 6

1. ADVICE TO CHILDREN AND PARENTS—Paul's advice to children and parents is both measured and wise. If it were followed, parent-child relationships would be more harmonious. Of course, some contentiousness can be present in even the best of families. Still, The Apostle is telling us: "Be respectful of each other."

2. THE FULL ARMOR OF GOD—The Apostle knows the ferocity of spiritual attacks. Supernatural assaults require stronger than normal defenses. In this most profound section of Ephesians 6, Paul helps us visualize the eternal armor available to human beings as they face assaults from demonic forces.

3. CALLING OUT EVIL—Paul identifies the true origin and devilish power of our attackers. Most people fail to perceive threats originating from invisible sources. It can be a hard concept to fathom: the unseen power of evil targeting flesh and blood human beings.

The Apostle confirms this dark reality and how we can confront it.

4. THE IMPORTANCE OF WITHSTANDING SPIRITUAL ATTACKS—Paul understands the importance of "standing" strong on the spiritual battlefield. If evil manages to erase even one soul from the fray, it lessens the number of warriors under God's command. The Apostle highlights the crucial importance of every soul in the struggle to overcome evil.

5. IDENTIFYING THE BELT OF TRUTH—What is the "Belt of Truth"? From a metaphysical standpoint, it can mean the eternal and never changing nature of God Itself. The material world is ever shifting and subject to constant highs and lows. God's eternal universe stands rooted on the Holy Ground of unchanging values. The Truth of Spirit can often be hidden beneath the world's glitter. We must become surrounded and encircled by God's clarity. Then, we can center ourselves in God's sacred Truth.

6. REMEMBERING THE BREASTPLATE OF RIGHTEOUSNESS—Paul wants us to understand the importance of righteousness as part of our full armor. God asks that we practice righteous behavior in our daily lives. If we stand for anything, let it be the "Good" that exists around us. In a world consumed by unrighteous thoughts and actions, we can offer the countervailing force in keeping the planet on a positive path.

7. THE IMPORTANCE OF KEEPING OUR FEET FITTED WITH THE READINESS THAT COMES FROM THE GOSPEL OF PEACE—We must always be prepared to move forward spiritually. There are many times when speedy action can mean the difference between life and death. If our movements become frozen and paralyzed with fear, we may miss the opportunity to escape from a spiritual attack. The Holy Word of God keeps our feet at the ready.

8. HOW THE SHIELD OF FAITH SUSTAINS US—Anytime we feel threatened by anyone or anything, we must reach for the impenetrable shield forged for us

by God. When the world threatens to overwhelm us, bring up the shield of Faith to safely cover your face and body. Let the flaming arrows fall away. A Faith made of steel protects, sustains, and encourages us when we encounter evil. Surely, we will live to fight another day, protected by God's Holy Armor.

9. PRESERVING OUR VULNERABLE MINDS WITH THE HELMET OF SALVATION—Many of the devil's most cunning and baffling attacks are directed at our human brains. Our minds can become infected with hate, anger, and resentment. We can develop tumors of prejudice and bigotry. Negative thinking warps our logic and reasoning. We must be sure our spiritual Helmet is firmly in place before getting derailed by a lack of clarity, forgiveness and understanding. Removing dangerous thinking from our minds calls for awareness and immediate action.

10. CUTTING THROUGH THE CHAFF OF LIFE WITH THE SWORD OF THE SPIRIT. We can use the sharp-edged sword of God's Holy Word to help us chop through the distractions of human life. In the pages of the Bible, we are given a helpful guide for living a successful life. Because it is such an ancient document, we may tend to question the Bible's relevance to modern life. Nothing could be more wrong. In these sacred pages, we are handed an invaluable roadmap that keeps us steered away from the gates of hell. Reading and meditating on God's Word helps us separate the nurturing wheat from the meaningless chaff.

11. THE NECESSITY OF CONTINUOUS PRAYER—Paul urges us to pray without ceasing. He says that God wants our prayers, both big and small. When he instructs human beings to "pray in the spirit on all occasions", The Apostle underlines how prayer can solidify our divine connection with God. He also requests prayer for himself as well,

asking that inspired words flow to him as he toils as "an ambassador in Chains" on behalf of God and Jesus.

12. A VISUALIZATION OF GOOD BEING ABLE TO SURVIVE SPIRITUAL ATTACKS—The "Full Armor of God" offers God's followers a powerful visualization—that you and I can be protected. We can survive the ferocious attacks by evil that may come our way. Our spiritual backers, namely God, Jesus, and The Apostle Paul understand the vulnerability of human beings. We need an extra layer of divine protection against the flaming arrows that fly our way.

BELINDA'S QUANDARY

Belinda Jordan was wired for happiness, joy and a problem-free life. The Dallas native was a sixth-grade teacher at the same Highland Park Middle School that she had attended two decades earlier. Some of her classmates from back then had proceeded on to considerable fame and riches. One was a longtime NFL quarterback. Another was the best pitcher in the major leagues and a recent MVP in the World Series. She could still watch her best girlfriend from the 7th grade every week on TV in a long running series. Countless others were big shots in the corporate world, especially high tech. At least one techie chum was a billionaire several times over and a household name. Her boyfriend Rob from those days (he later graduated from the St. Marks prep school) went on to Harvard for his undergraduate degree. He came back home to do his legal studies at the SMU School of Law. Rob now worked in downtown Dallas for the largest law firm in the entire state. Belinda had received an education degree from the University of Texas at Austin and relocated back to Dallas when a job emerged at her middle school alma mater. She had recently been named "Teacher of the Year" for the entire Highland Park school district. Belinda and Rob had been happily married for 10 years. Their wedding reception was held at his parent's magnificent home across the street from an ex-president (who had walked across the street to attend). The couple had been blessed by a pair of rich and generous parents, both of whom doted on the Jordan's two children—Rob III (8) and Helaine (6). The grandparents had recently chipped in to buy a home for the couple near Armstrong Parkway in the heart of Highland Park. The Jordan's coffers were full. Life was beyond good. It was perfect.

Then, something happened with Belinda. The Jordan Family attended the Highland Park United Methodist Church. The venerable old church had been around for more than 100 years. It was a religious pillar for the entire city. The church's religious presence had impacted the community over the decades in many positive ways. One of its long-time members had coached the local NFL team for decades before his passing. He and other leaders had influenced many people to seek a relationship with Jesus Christ. Belinda herself now taught Sunday School at the church, just like the Hall of Fame coach had done for many years. One day at a regular Sunday service, the senior pastor had referenced scripture written by the Apostle Paul in his letter to the Ephesians. From Ephesians 5:8-14, the minister had read these words to the congregation: "For you were once darkness, but now you are light in the Lord. Live as children of light. For the fruit of the light consists in all goodness, righteousness and truth. Find out what pleases the Lord. Have nothing to do with the fruitless deeds of darkness, but instead expose them. Wake up, sleeper. Rise from the dead and Christ will shine on you." When she heard these words, Belinda felt a sudden surge of adrenalin explode throughout her body. She had difficulty breathing. The unexpected episode startled and concerned her. "Am I about to pass out right here in the middle of church and embarrass myself and my family?" she thought to herself. Then, from somewhere behind her, she heard these words in a whispered but clear voice: "I will never leave you. I will never forsake you. Just breathe." Belinda took several deep breaths and the adrenalin surge subsided. As she left the sanctuary that morning, she did not mention what had happened to anyone.

For the next few days, she debated whether to query someone at the church about the experience. Belinda waited until the following Sunday before singling out a young assistant minister who was about her own age. She explained what had occurred and asked what he thought. The assistant pastor appeared startled. "Belinda, that is the exact same scripture that made me decide to enter the ministry. I felt like God was talking to me through Paul. I was majoring in business at UT-Dallas and about to graduate. I was not particularly enthused about spending the rest of my life in the corporate world. Then I came to church here one Sunday and heard that passage from the Bible. It changed my life. I applied at the Perkins School of Theology at SMU and the rest is history. God could be trying to get your attention. I would not discount it. We get messages from God all of the time."

Belinda went home that day and strolled outside to her spacious patio. Rob had taken the kids out for burgers and she was alone. Her first thoughts were about the perfect life that she enjoyed. Everything had fallen into place with little effort on her part. She had been blessed with the perfect parents, the perfect husband, the perfect children, the perfect home, the perfect job, the perfect friends and on it went. She bowed her head and asked God for clarification. Seeking divine guidance was something she rarely did. But this time Belinda needed a connection with her Higher Power. God did not disappoint. From deep within herself, Belinda detected a still, small voice. "I've been waiting for you," the voice said, "I AM here to support you, guide you and love you. Yes, I have called your name. You did not choose Me. I chose you. I have specific work that only you can do. I gave you a special talent for spreading My word across the landscape. Just as I did with Paul, I have some traveling I want you to do in My Name. There is an important job that needs your attention. I have prepared you to take on this assignment. Please do not panic and say no without even considering My request. If you accept My will, your spiritual service can change the world for the better. I would call that a pretty big deal."

Belinda felt almost trapped. Here she was, having a personal conversation with God about something she did not understand or comprehend. "But I already have a perfect life," Belinda told the voice, "Why would I want to change it? I did not study to be a minister. I teach school and I like it-- a lot. I also have a big job as mother to my children and wife to Rob. I could never leave them. I do not understand what special talent I might offer you. My voice is not good enough to even sing in the church choir. With all due respect, I think you have the wrong person. I can't be a candidate for any job different from the ones I already have."

Belinda thought she heard a chuckle from the small voice within her. "That is what they all say," It said. "You have to understand," Spirit continued, "Your teaching career has helped prepare you for what I have in mind. The assignment involves organizing and evangelizing children all around the world. Remember what Jesus proclaimed: "If you want to find salvation, you must become as a little child." I want the young ones to know Me before they get corrupted by the material world. You will act as one of the lead teachers in the Children's Spiritual Movement. You are the perfect human vessel to act as My divine instrument. In doing so, you will fulfill your life destiny.'

Belinda had heard enough. She leaped to her feet and stalked off the patio and back into the house. "If God thinks I would leave my perfect life to lead a Children's Crusade, He is dead wrong," she thought, "I would never consider it." Later that same night, the Angel Gabriel visited her in a dream. The Messenger Angel reiterated God's comments about Belinda being the right and perfect person for the assignment with the children. In the dream, Belinda listened patiently for a time, but then began shouting "No, no, no." She realized that her shouts had spilled over into the real world when Rob called out "What's the matter, Bel? What are you saying "No, no, no about? That must have been some nightmare. You will be OK. Go back to sleep."

For the next several days, Belinda tried not to think about these strange happenings. But the next Sunday at church, the young pastor that she had spoken to earlier sought her out. "I've been praying about you," he said, "I'm hearing some strange things. I think God has picked you for some sort of important job. Have you heard anything?". Without hesitation, Belinda shared about the still, small voice and the dream featuring the

Angel Gabriel. The minister did not seem surprised. "I had a dream this week too," he said. "This dream was not so good. It was more like a nightmare. I pictured you surrounded by swirling clouds of pure evil. I do not want to frighten you, Belinda, but these creatures were demon like. They were ferocious. They kept attacking you. You were trying to fight back, but the demons were winning. It was scary. I had debated whether to share those images with you today. I am still not sure if it is a good idea. The Apostle Paul was also in my dream, standing right next to you. He kept telling you to put on the full armor of God so that you could stand up to the evil doers."

Belinda felt almost sick to her stomach. She put up her hand as if asking the young pastor to stop sharing. Without a word, she turned and trooped into the sanctuary. She found Rob and the children already seated in a back pew. "What's the matter with you?" Rob asked in a worried voice. "You look flushed. What happened?" Belinda just shook her head and said: "I will tell you about it later."

When they returned home after church, Rob sent the kids outside to play. He and Belinda sat down in their large living room. She began crying while telling her husband about the strange events. Rob listened carefully, but soon began frowning. He started shaking his head. "Well, that's pretty damn crazy," he opined. "I always thought there was something funny about that young minister. I have never much cared for the guy. Promise me you will stay away from him." Bel nodded her head in agreement.

In fact, Belinda invented a reason to stay home from church the following Sunday. She dispatched Rob and the kids off without her. After they were gone, Bel strolled back into her living room and sat down in her favorite chair. She closed her eyes and prayed, "God, why are you upsetting me like this? You made me too scared to even go back to church today. What is happening? I do not like it. I have a great life. Will you please just leave me alone? I am not the person to lead a revolution of children or anybody. I love you, God, but will you please leave me alone? Please. I am begging you. Find somebody else to take this on."

For a long minute or too, the still small voice was quiet. I wonder if God is mad at me, Belinda thought. Then, she heard these words from the depth of her being: "I know you feel inadequate to answer My call. Virtually every person I summon to spiritual service always says no in the beginning. I understand your human reluctance and allow for it. You ask: "Why me, Lord". I am just a common everyday human being. What could I possibly offer to you?" Let me help you understand My thinking. Every soul is carefully molded. Each one possesses uncommon talents. I created you all in My image and likeness, but with unique gifts. I gave you special talents that you cannot imagine. If I AM calling you into spiritual service of any kind, I have equipped you with everything needed to complete the task. But allow Me to be honest with you, Belinda. My Path can be a hard one. When you agree to do what I ask, you will almost immediately begin experiencing losses. Your loved ones may think you are having a breakdown. Expect them to argue and even become angry with you. Pure Evil is already circling around you. It never stops attacking those who serve Me. If you agree to My Plan for you, expect serious assaults on you, your family, your profession, your friends and everything you hold dear. The Apostle Paul was spot on when he told you to put on the Full Armor of God. He knows all about how far evil will go to shut somebody down if they agree to follow Me. However, I do not want to scare you away. Those who march under My banner will find it a joyful and fulfilling journey, along with the hard challenges. But please hear Me, My child. I give you the Free Will choice to reject My offer. If you say no to My plan, you will go on living what you call the perfect life. You just never experience the ultimate satisfaction of changing the entire world for the better."

Belinda was touched by what she had heard. The "teacher" in her liked to excel at "tests". Surely this colossal opportunity from Spirit represented a different kind of "test". What should she do? For a long minute, she pondered all that had happened. Then Belinda Jordan took a deep breath and whispered, "OK, God, I will do it." Later, she would realize that her response came from a higher place in her consciousness. Somehow, she had tapped into a part of herself that had never been activated before. Belinda felt an immediate peace. Her entire body relaxed.

Ephesians 6

She felt encased in a protective bubble Then, without warning, she heard a loud explosion outside. I was much like a bomb going off. Belinda jumped up and raced to the picture window in her living room. There, in the middle of her street, a small single engine airplane had crashed. It was engulfed in flames. Chaos and confusion were everywhere.

"And so, it begins," she thought, "My life will never be the same, never ever be the same. What have I gotten myself into?"

Then, she heard the still, small voice once more. It was calm and reassuring. "Trust in Me, My child. I will never leave or forsake you. Now, quick, call 9-1-1."

MOST COMMON TYPES OF SPIRITUAL ATTACKS

SEX—CARNAL TEMPTATIONS ABOUND IN SPIRITUAL WARFARE

MONEY—WEALTH OFTEN SKEWS OUR PRIORITIES

POWER—EXERCISING CONTROL OVER OTHERS INVITES TROUBLE

FAME—SOME PEOPLE MISTAKENLY BELIEVE FAME LASTS FOREVER

ANGER—A DAMAGING EMOTION THAT ALWAYS CAUSES STRESS

RESENTMENT—ALLOWING OUR EGO TO BECOME JUDGE AND JURY

FALSE HUMILITY—PERMITTING SELF-RIGHTEOUSNESS TO RULE US

Ephesians 6

MY IDEA OF WHAT CONSTITUTES A SPIRITUAL ATTACK

_____

_____

_____

_____

_____

_____

_____

_____

CONCLUSION

Thank you for spending your time considering Ephesians 6, The Apostle Paul, and The Full Armor of God. No one knows when a spiritual attack may unfold from the Heavenly Realms around us. If it happens to you, do not panic. Take a deep breath. Then remember this little book. Start praying for God's help. Reach for The Full Armor of God as soon as possible. Put on every layer. Prepare to stand your ground. Know that you are never alone on the spiritual battlefield. God's resources are always available. Keep praying for divine assistance in turning away the forces of evil. Repeat these words: "If God is for me, who can be against me?" Cinch up your Belt of Truth. Lift high the Shield of Faith. Reach for the Sword of God's Word, the Holy Bible. Let it protect and save you from the sharp-edged thrusts of evil. Let God's Full Armor protect and embolden you. Nothing can harm you now. Believe it.

Oh, by the way. Before you go, the Apostle Paul has asked for a word with you. There some loose ends he wants to tie up before you head back into your material life. It will not take long.

Thank you, again, dear reader. Always remember who you are: a beloved and powerful child of the Most-High God. Being a warrior of the Spirit constitutes your destiny. It is why you are still here.

A FEW LAST WORDS FROM PAUL

Thank you for spending time with my letter to the churches around Ephesus. Without a doubt, this epistle remains one of my all-time favorites. And, before you ask, yes, I did write it myself while I was in jail in Rome. Many so-called "scholars" tell people that the letter was a summary written by some sort of committee 20 years later. Baloney! It was all me. It is not about my ego, although I am quite proud of the language. I put my guts and soul into every word. Of course, you focused on Chapter 6 and the section about putting on the full armor of God. Some educated people do not believe in spiritual attacks. I will admit the concept may be hard to grasp. Then you behold a flaming arrow headed your way. Hear me out! Pure evil can be much more subtle and deadlier than you think. It often appears in the most beautiful of packages. The Devil loves catching God's followers asleep or distracted. When you deal with the "cunning and baffling" darkness of real evil, you can get chewed up before you know it. Trust me! I have been tested by all of it, the direct and the indirect thrusts of the dark side. Do not get me wrong! I never once enjoyed being beaten with rods! But without a doubt, the tricky stuff that sneaks up on you can be much worse. You must always trust God's Armor when the crunch time arrives. I promise you that it will someday arrive, most times when you least expect it. Most unsuspecting human beings think they are in control of their life. Then, boom! Everything changes in an instant. You are caught in a full spin. But I wanted to visit with you for another reason. In the letter to the Ephesians, I tried to make a specific point about relationships in general. Please listen. Try to understand what I am saying. It concerns the true meaning of life. I can sum it all up in six words: "God wants everybody to get along". Can it be any simpler? God wants every living thing to co-exist with each other in harmony and good will. That means getting along on the most basic level. It means no more wars and personal battles with people you see as being different from yourself. Spirit asks that you look outside of obvious differences like gender, age, skin color, and language. Religion, politics, and sexual preference also can act as "separators". God insists that you should never hate someone for their outer appearances or personal choices. Here is the Truth with a capital "T". God created every one of us alike in the ways that matter. We have hearts that are programmed to love, be compassionate and care about our fellow human beings. We can live in an ongoing state of forgiveness with each other. Most all of us are born into families. If we are lucky, a family structure can offer instant acceptance, needed protection and unconditional love. Of course, I know that too many families do not measure up to those standards, especially these days. The world is testing everyone right now. That is why God wants you to know something important. The Holy Spirit that God placed inside of you acts as your family of last resort. You are never alone or forsaken. God worries a lot about people feeling unloved and abandoned. That can lead to them not caring about others. When you do not worry about the fate of someone else, it makes harming them easier. The Devil loves it when things get to that point. That brings me back to why I wanted one last word with you. Please make a conscious decision to love, appreciate and get along with others.

Of course, people see things differently. Allow for that. Be gentle with your judgements. But hear me on this point: you should never tolerate abuse from anyone. Try to walk the earth as a healing light, not as a hateful spark that can be ignited into a blazing fire. God put us all here to serve each other. Do your part. Find your reward in making things better for everyone. Thank you for your time. Forgive me if I slipped over into preaching. That's what I do."

NOTES

ABOUT THE AUTHOR

Rev. Allen C. Liles is a graduate of Baylor University in Waco, TX and the Unity School of Religious Studies in Unity Village, MO. Before being ordained as a non-denominational minister in 1993, he served as vice-president of public relations for The Southland Corporation (7-Eleven) in Dallas, TX and communications manager for The McLane Company in Temple, TX. Rev. Liles was also Senior Director for Outreach at Unity Village from 1995-2001 and served as senior minister at Unity churches in Missouri, Arizona and Minnesota.

BOOKS BY ALLEN C. LILES:

John 14: The Most Important Book in the New Testament

Sitting With God/Meditating for God's Divine Guidance

The 7 Puzzles of Life/God's Plan to Save the World

The Forever Penny/How Our Loved Ones Stay Connected After Death

Oh Thank Heaven! The Story of the Southland Corporation

E-BOOKS ON www.smashwords.com

The 12 Promises of Heaven

Friends of Jesus

E-Spiritual Rehab

The Book of Celeste/God Recruits a Blogger

The Book of Floyd/God Transforms a Racist

The Book of Ethan/God Confronts Teen Suicide

ON AUDIBLE:

The Peaceful Driver/Steering Clear of Road Rage

www.ingramcontent.com/pod-product-compliance
Lightning Source LLC
Chambersburg PA
CBHW052109110526
44592CB00013B/1539